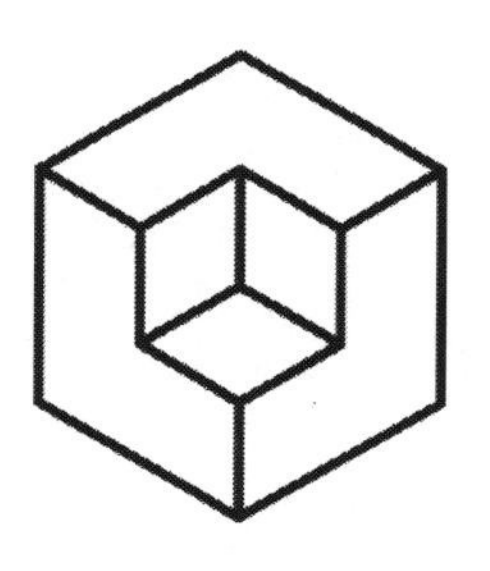

ESSENTIAL CHURCH:

RETURNING TO WHAT MATTERS MOST

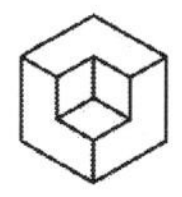

Brady Boyd
Glenn Packiam
Daniel Grothe
Andrew Arndt

New Life Church
11025 Voyager Parkway
Colorado Springs, CO 80921

New Life Church
11025 Voyager Parkway
Colorado Springs, CO 80921
www.newlifechurch.org

Cover/Layout - Fernweh Creative

Essential Church: Returning to what matters most / Brady Boyd, Glenn Packiam, Daniel Grothe, Andrew Arndt. —1st ed.

ISBN 978-0-692-18241-3

Contents

CHAPTER 1

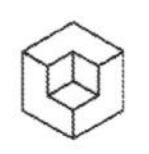

CHURCH AS HOME

{God is building a home}

He's using us all—irrespective of how we got here—in what he is building. He used the apostles and prophets for the foundation. Now he's using you, fitting you in brick by brick, stone by stone, with Christ Jesus as the cornerstone that holds all the parts together. We see it taking shape day after day—a holy temple built by God, all of us built into it, a temple in which God is quite at home.

—EPHESIANS 2.20-22, MSG[1]

[1] All Scriptures are taken from *The Message*, unless otherwise noted.

TO KNOW A thing's *essence* is to understand the fundamentals of that thing. It is to recognize the irreducible ingredients that make it what it is, those things that, once removed, cause the thing to no longer be that thing. It is to apprehend its identity. To pick it out from all the other things. To grasp, as philosophers of old would say of a thing, "the what it was to be."[2]

We see "essence" in nature: Without sea life and salt water and waves, for example, what would the ocean be? A lake, maybe? A pond? *Essential* to an ocean are these designations; these mark the essence of an ocean's existence. They are what separate an ocean from other bodies of water.

Likewise, *essential* to a tree are roots and stems and leaves.

Essential to the sky are sun and moon and stars.

Essential to summertime are long days, vacations, and warmth.

We see "essence" in the marketplace: What would Starbucks be without coffee? What would McDonald's be without cheeseburgers? What would Ford Motor Company be without trucks?

We see "essence" in daily life. What is a smartphone without a cell signal? What is a weekend without a little time off? Closer to home for Coloradans, what is a ski run without fresh powder, besides a very long walk in the woods?

We see this idea of *essence* nearly everywhere we look, and it's this concept that tells us what we're looking at—what it is, what it's not, how it's unique. And so, as we begin this conversation about New Life Church—who we are, who we're not, why we say and

[2] Aristotle, Plato, others. https://en.wikipedia.org/wiki/Essence

do the things we say and do—it's only fitting to begin by answering the central question: *What is the essence of the church*? In other words, what are those things that are *so essential* to this entire thing called "church," the global and historical church that has existed for 2,000 years across culture and geography, and thus *so essential* to us, that to remove them would compromise our very identity as God's people?

. . .

As this chapter's epigraph from Ephesians declared, God is building a home. This project has been underway since the days of Adam and Eve, and, demonstrating his unbelievable tenacity, God *still* has not tired of the work. Much like a doting mother during the holidays, God's dream for this home is that all his children would gather together, compelled by passion and unified by love. His vision is that we'd fit *together*, instead of ripping apart at the seams. His dream is a massive, active portrait … of a family, at home, with him.

He would name this family *beloved*, his *children*, his *image-bearing called-out ones*. And his Son, Jesus, too would fight for this dream, for a family, at home, with God. "Church," he would name this family. *Church of the living God.*

In the Gospel of Matthew, Chapter 16, we find an interesting scene. It's the 1st century and Jesus' ministry is well underway—attracting large crowds from all over Galilee and Judea to witness his preaching, teaching, and healing. He has come to the region of Caesarea Philippi, his disciples are with him, and he asks them, "What are people saying about who the Son of Man is?"(Jesus, by the way, is the Son of Man. This is not really a trick question.)

The disciples have an answer for him. "Some think he is John the Baptizer," they say, "some say Elijah, some Jeremiah or one of the other prophets …" to which Jesus says, "And how about you? Who do *you* say I am?"

Simon Peter answers first. "You're the Christ," he replies, "the Messiah, the Son of the living God."

Exactly right.

"God bless you, Simon!" Jesus says to him. "You didn't get that answer out of books or from teachers. My Father in heaven, God himself, let you in on this secret of who I really am. And now I'm going to tell you who you are, who you *really* are. You are Peter, a rock. This is the rock on which I will put together my church, a church so expansive with energy that not even the gates of hell will be able to keep it out."

> *"My family will be so strong, so resilient, so durable," Jesus was saying, "that the very worst that hell can offer, its selfishness and hatred and rage, its bent toward destruction and gnashing of teeth, its perversion and wickedness and vitriol…even these forces won't bring it down" (Matthew 16:13-18).*

And if history has demonstrated one thing thus far, it's that this divine dream has proven remarkably resilient. Across culture and geography, across time and space, from the 1st century until our own 21st century, *the church of Jesus Christ has stood the test of time.* His church will *always* stand that test.

Mighty empires have risen and fallen; great thinkers and leaders and artists and musicians have come and gone; fads, fashions, and philosophies all have had their day … but there is one institution that has endured: *the church of Jesus Christ,* "expansive with energy" until he returns once more. God's home is being built—by people just like us, in cooperation with God's Spirit.

The question that remains is: *Will we join him in that noble work, or will we pursue lesser dreams?*

. . .

When Jesus returned to heaven following his three-year ministry here on earth, he tasked his followers with a mission—a practical, tactical way to keep God's divine dream alive. According to Matthew 28:18-20, there before his disciples that day, he put it this way: "God authorized and commanded me to commission you: Go out and train everyone you meet, far and near, in this way of life, marking them by baptism in the threefold name: Father, Son, and Holy Spirit. Then instruct them in the practice of all I have commanded you. I'll be with you as you do this, day after day after day, right up to the end of the age" (vv. 18-20)

"Take *all* that I have taught you," Jesus was saying, "to *all* the people you meet. Teach those people. Encourage those people. Serve them and tell them of me. Love them well. Enfold them in the fellowship. Regard them as the *family members* they are." In Jesus' estimation, the grand goal for our lives here on earth is to become co-dreamers and co-actors, if you will, with God. We are to set our sights on pushing back darkness, ushering in redemption, and healing the world he adores.

And then, perhaps most importantly, Jesus issues a needed reminder: "I'll be with you," he assures us, "as you do this, day after day after day . . ."

. . .

Jesus promises such companionship for many reasons. Surely one reason is comfort. He knows that the work will often be hard, and we'll need his tender, life-giving presence as we work with and for him. But another reason is this: he knows how prone we are to *drift*.

On a stormy night in 1992, a cargo ship crossing the Pacific Ocean lost one of its forty-foot-long steel shipping crates overboard. The crate, on its way from the United States to Hong Kong, was full of children's bath toys—blue turtles, green frogs, and yellow rubber ducks.

Upon sinking to the bottom of the ocean, the crate popped open and began to release its contents, which is when approximately thirty thousand turtles, frogs, and ducks floated upward to the surface of the ocean. Days and weeks, months and years, went by as the ocean's tides and currents and winds carried those toys quite literally to the four corners of the earth. Along the way, yellow rubber duckies were spotted floating along the site where the *Titanic* sank. They washed ashore in Japan, Alaska, and Hawaii. Some made it as far as Newfoundland and Scotland. At least one was found frozen in arctic ice. *That's a long way from home*. The ducks fell prey to the power and peril of *drift*.

Around New Life, when we think about God's original dream—all his children, united by love, enjoying fellowship together in his home—and about the societal, cultural, spiritual, and emotional tides and currents today that threaten to keep that dream from coming true, it compels us to re-up our commitment. We're determined to avoid the peril of drift. We are committed to doing exactly what Jesus told us to do, for God's glory and the world's good, slicing through the winds of fad and fashion so that the dream of God would be realized in our time.

In coming chapters, we'll detail these commitments—to Jesus, his gospel, the Scriptures, and more—but let's first look at four values we hold as a church that mark us out and help us "stand against the tide" of cultural pressure.

The church of Jesus Christ prizes diversity.

To be human is to long to be with people who look, think, talk, and vote like we do; truly, this "tribal" mentality is hardwired into our DNA. Before the rise of modern civilizations, human beings found identity and purpose not just *primarily* but *exclusively* through family, clan, and tribe. People who looked like you, thought like you, and talked like you—that was your entire world, and this wasn't necessarily a bad thing. Family, clan, and tribe provided safety and security. They provided a place of belonging. They surrounded you with love. But as civilizations evolved, the need for tribes changed. Or it *should* have changed, anyway. For many, the craving for exclusive homogeneity still drives their attitudes and ways. Even in this modern, globalized, "boundaryless" world, many of us tend to retreat into safe and familiar patterns of engagement with others who are like us in order to feel safe and secure and loved. We tend to cave to like-me preferences. We tend to retreat into the familiarity of tribe.

Many sociologists and social commentators think that tribalism is reaching staggeringly new proportions in our society. *New York Times* columnist David Brooks has argued that in many ways, we have *regressed* in the generations since the Civil Rights movement led by Dr. Martin Luther King, Jr. and others. Whereas Dr. King emphasized our common *humanity*, many today are appealing instead to a *common enemy*. And who is that enemy? *Whoever is not in our tribe,* whichever tribe that may be. "The problem," Brooks writes, "is that tribal common-enemy thinking tears a diverse nation apart."[3] When the forces that divide us are greater than the forces that unite us, hatred, envy, suspicion, strife, and even violence are the likely result. Which is, sadly, exactly what we see written across our headlines and in our neighborhoods most every day.

Tribalistic thinking can even creep into the local church. Years ago, Dr. King famously said that eleven o'clock on a Sunday morning was the most segregated hour in America—and little has changed since then. Add to that racial dividing line the divisions of politics, economics, and more, and trouble *really* starts to brew.

Tragically, in response to these dynamics, many churches just gave up the fight. "Like attracts like," the thinking went, "so we'll just organize ourselves around our kind." And so those church leaders reinforced with

---

[3] https://mobile.nytimes.com/2018/01/01/opinion/the-retreat-to-tribalism.html

permanent marker the lines they saw, moved on, and never looked back. Which would have been a fine approach to take … except that *the Bible says it is not.*

In several places throughout the New Testament[4], the apostle Paul claimed that because of Jesus' redemptive work on the cross, in which the full weight of our sin was dealt with, bridging the gap between God and humanity that that sin had laid wide, it was no longer appropriate to speak of "us" and a "them." No longer was there a barrier between Jew and Greek, or between male and female, or between slave and free. The identity that Christ secured for *all* who would believe—Jews, Greeks, males, females, slaves, and free alike—was *beloved,* God's son, God's daughter, God's friend. It was this vision that compelled God to declare to the great patriarch of the Jewish faith, Abraham, that he would be the "father of many nations" (Genesis 17:5) meaning "the father of many." One giant family—beloved by the Lord.

Christ's work on the cross makes room in the family of God for people from every nation, tribe, and language, as Revelation 7:9 says, creating the conditions for a raucous, everlasting, multi-ethnic, multi-lingual worship service to ensue. Which is precisely what we aim for at New Life Church. We welcome *all* people—regardless of gender, age, background, ethnicity, voting record, socioeconomic status, or any of a thousand other lines of demarcation our fallen human nature is tempted to draw—into our living room, the place where we worship God.

---

[4] Galatians 3:28, Ephesians 2:14, Colossians 2:11.

The church of Jesus Christ prizes authenticity.

Life is hard and full of challenge. It makes sense, then, for people who set foot inside of a church to think, "I'll stay, as long as you don't add to the burden I already bear …"

People who feel stressed don't want to subject themselves to further stressors still. They want to feel uplifted. They want to feel inspired. They want to feel encouraged. They want to know relief. The last thing they want to do is to "give up an hour on Sunday morning" for something that seems indicting, demanding, or hard.

Now, to be sure, we at New Life work to encourage one another, as the writer of Hebrews said to do in Hebrews 10:24-25, so that we are equipped to face the challenges of earthly life with faith instead of fear. Indeed, this is a big part of what it means to be the body of Christ, but this encouragement *must be grounded in truth*. "Who needs a doctor: the healthy or the sick?" Jesus asked in Luke 5:31.

What Jesus is saying is that we aren't merely *discouraged* people in need of a pep talk; we are *fatally diseased* people who need to be healed. We are sinners who need to repent. We are the walking dead in search of true life.

Think of it this way: If you head to the doctor to try to sort out a severe pain you've been experiencing, the last thing you want to hear is, "Wow! That pain must be awful to bear! But I believe in you! I just know you're going to do great. Good luck to you, champ! It'll all work out—you'll see!" You didn't come looking for encouragement; you came *looking for healing*. And in the same way that the healing you seek likely requires ears to hear straight talk on the errant habits you've indulged that have led to the unhealthy processes at work in your body, the self-discipline required to right some lifestyle wrongs, and the kind of commitment you'll need to stay the course the doctor lays out, so your spiritual healing comes by a combination of truth-telling, humility, and personal tenacity to see the healing through.

Yes, it is certainly nice when the doctor delivers the necessary information with compassion and tenderness and care. "Bedside manner" is crucial. Likewise, we strive for this same gentle touch at New Life, *even as we're committed to telling the truth*. Our hope is that you'll find such authenticity refreshing.

The church of Jesus Christ prizes generosity.

Despite the bad rap that the local church often gets for being "money-hungry," our goal at New Life, simply put, is to call believers—who are not *donors*, but *worshipers,* by the way—to God's standard for generosity as outlined in Scripture. From beginning to end, God's Word declares that our financial resources are *gifts from God* to be stewarded for God's glory and the world's good. To the biblical mind, across both Old and New Testaments, giving generously, selflessly, and sacrificially to the local fellowship of believers is part of that stewardship.

Examples of this theme abound, including the following:

- Abraham gave a tenth of his spoils to Melchizedek (Genesis 14:18-20).
- The prophet Malachi said that the people were "robbing God" by withholding tithes and offerings (Malachi 3:6-9).
- The poor widow threw all she had to live on into the temple offering (Mark 12:41-44).
- In the early church, no one claimed their possessions were their own and every-one shared freely all they had with one another (Acts 4:32-35).

In these and other passages, financial giving is first a *Godward* act. It is an expression of *worship*. That's what makes disciples different from mere *donors*. Far from pursuing one's "pet passion" through giving, disciples give as a way of surrendering their lives and resources *completely* to God. It is a way of saying, "Not my will, but yours be done."

Along these lines, Jesus founded the local church and intended for his followers to support the church with generous gifts, each as he or she was able. Financial gifts in the New Testament were understood as an intrinsic part of discipleship and a joyful response to the Spirit's work and were directed to the local fellowships in each city, where a group of leaders oversaw the use and distribution of those resources.

At New Life, we believe that part of the task that Jesus has laid at our feet is to help people see their financial resources as "instruments of worship" that connect them to causes and projects with which they may never be personally involved. When approached this way, giving becomes genuinely *sacrificial, self-denying*, and *worshipful* … rather than *self-serving, grudging,* and *chore-like*.

When the cycle of giving is working well, believers give joyfully, distribute resources wisely, embrace accountability and transparency thoroughly, and see to it that needs are met.

The church of Jesus Christ prizes community.

You've probably attended a large-scale concert or a professional sporting event at some point, and so you know that few things are more fun and inspiring than getting caught up with thousands of other fans in the sheer elation of soul-stirring music or the achievements of your team. When the music reaches its crescendo, when the team scores the winning touchdown, when strangers sing together at the top of their lungs or exchange high-fives—there's just something about it, right? Such experiences stir the soul, even as they, inevitably, come to an end.

When the concert or the sporting event is over, when the final note has been played or the clock shows "00:00", your connection to those thousands of people is lost—a moment in time that fades into oblivion and makes no lasting contribution to the shape and substance of your life. You entered the arena with hundreds or thousands of others as strangers, and you leave it as strangers. Nothing has changed.

But in the local church, God's dream is that the connection would remain. Yes, we may enter it as strangers, but as the Spirit draws us to one another, we leave it as friends, as *family*. In 1 Corinthians 12:13, the apostle Paul wrote, "For by one Spirit we were all baptized into one body"—which is the very body of Christ. We've been made members together of one body, sharers in and of the person of Christ—a reality *way* bigger than a concert or a sporting event.

Because of this reality, it makes sense that the New Testament metaphors that speak of the church refer not to an individual, but to a *gathering* of called-out ones. For example, believers are called:

- the family/household of God *(1 Timothy 3:15)*;
- the body of Christ *(1 Corinthians 12:27)*;
- the temple of the Holy Spirit *(Ephesians 2:21-22)*;
- a colony of heaven *(Philippians 3:20)*;
- the people of God *(Ephesians 2:19)*;
- a holy nation *(1 Peter 2:9)*; and,
- the city of the living God *(Hebrews 12:22)*.

Even the Greek word for church itself—"ekklesia"—in the 1st century referred to a civic assembly. The concept of church is inescapably corporate; "anonymous Christian" is a contradiction in terms. To follow Jesus is to belong *both* to the God he called "Father" *and* to the people who bear his name. Paul says in Romans 12:5 that in Christ we, though many, form one body, and that *each member belongs to all the others*. This means that *by definition*, to be part of the church is to have our lives increasingly woven into the tapestry of love and humility, openness and vulnerability, care and support, that is the family of God. Yes, this means we'll get messy. (Humans are messy, every one of us.) Yes, this will require vulnerability. (Can true relationship be built another way?) Yes, we'll want to isolate and insulate each time we suffer a relational fall. (Wherever two or three are gathered, someone will inevitably say something that offends.) But if we long for the healing Christ promises, then we will persevere with those who are sick. We will stay the course with others and trust that they'll stay the course with us.

In a society that is traumatized and isolated, fractured and fragmented, lonely and fast losing hope, around New Life we believe that the time is now for us to rise again as the *body* of Christ, the *family* of God, where strangers become friends, outsiders become family, and orphans find a forever home.

CHAPTER 2

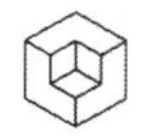

CHRIST, THE CENTER

This mystery has been kept in the dark for a long time, but now it's out in the open. God wanted everyone, not just Jews, to know this rich and glorious secret inside and out, regardless of their background, regardless of their religious standing.

The mystery in a nutshell is just this: Christ is in you, so therefore you can look forward to sharing in God's glory. It's that simple. That is the substance of our Message. We preach Christ, warning people not to add to the Message ...

Christ! No more, no less ...

—COLOSSIANS 1.28-29

THE LOCAL CHURCH is called to be a community that sweeps wayward sons and daughters up in its wake of redemptive, holy love. We want to see people saved and delivered and equipped for ministry, both in the church and in the world. But if we are not careful, we will find ourselves succumbing to the many pressures that our society is putting on us. When we do so, our churches become barely distinguishable from the world around us. When we start relying on *gimmickry rather than good news*, our churches start looking less like a gathering of the "citizens of high heaven," as Philippians 3:20 calls us, and more like weekly rock concerts, TED talk gatherings, or pep rallies with a little "Jesus cheer" sprinkled in at the end.

When we value gimmickry above the good news of Christ, we lose our focus on the reason we gather in the first place—namely, to worship him.

One of our pastors knew of a group of women in another state who had been praying for an unbelieving friend of theirs to come to faith in Jesus. The unbelieving friend finally agreed to attend a church service with them. Unfortunately, things didn't unfold as her friends had hoped. Not only was the name of Jesus never mentioned during that service, but no invitation to know him was extended, which meant that (in the worship gathering, at least) this woman would not meet Jesus that day.

To make it worse, while Jesus didn't make it into the service plans for that weekend, evidently, *beach balls* did. You read that right: Apparently, to "hype up" the crowd that Sunday morning, the worship leader tossed out a dozen or so beach balls, which the congregation then cheerfully batted around. And so this woman, who perhaps would have opened her heart to Jesus that morning, found herself clobbered by a beach ball instead.

Now, don't miss the point here. We think that church should be a place of lightheartedness, celebration, and joy. In the words of the psalmist, we are to come and "shout praises to God," to "raise the roof for the Rock who saved us," and to "march into his presence singing praises," and to "lift the rafters with our hymns!" (Psalms 95:1-2). Make no mistake: Joy is a *hallmark* of the people of God, but we mustn't elevate even joy above Jesus, the joy-giver himself.

The great 20th Christian writer C. S. Lewis (best known for *The Chronicles of Narnia* series) once put it like this: "Aim at Heaven and you will get earth 'thrown in'; aim at earth and you will get neither."[5] Indeed, one of the biggest mistakes that churches make is making some aspect of following Jesus or some benefit of following Jesus more important than Jesus himself. Things such as:

- Joy
- Beauty
- Justice
- Excellence
- Community
- Worship forms
- Preaching styles
- Doctrinal distinctives
- Charismatic personalities
- Gifts of the Spirit
- Obedience/keeping "the rules"
- Leadership

The list could go on—and again, these are not bad things. Far from it. They are good things, each and every one of them. They're just not higher than Jesus. They are not more important than Jesus. They must never take Jesus' place. The apostle Paul once

[5] C. S. Lewis. *Mere Christianity* (San Francisco: Harper, 2001), 134.

cautioned the Corinthian believers along these lines, saying, "I'm afraid that exactly as the Snake seduced Eve with his smooth patter, you are being lured away from the simple purity of your love for Christ" (2 Corinthians 11:3). Another translation renders the phrase "the simple purity of your love for Christ" this way: *the simplicity of your devotion to Christ.*

Purity of love.
Simplicity of love.
Devotion, which implies singlemindedness … *focused intent.*

This is what we're committed to at New Life. We're determined to be a church that is radically bound to the task of keeping Jesus central *to all* and *in all* that we do. In a time when it is easier and easier to make a *mascot* out of Jesus, we're bent on making him *here* what he in fact is, always, everywhere:

The Alpha and the Omega
The Beginning and the End
The Substance of all things

The Word of God
Name Above All Names
Son of God

King of Kings
Lord of Lords
Center of it all.

. . .

Jesus is the great Goal to which all of life has always been headed, the One in whom all things find their ultimate completion, the principal Actor on history's grand stage, the Hero of this drama called *life*. For these reasons, we at New Life believe that the message that God wants to convey about himself and his commitment to us is rooted fully and always in the person of Christ.

When we are struggling with sin, failure or doubt, God says over us: "Jesus."

When we wonder whether God loves us and has a plan for us, he says over us: "Jesus."

When we find ourselves awash in questions about the justice of the world around us, whether the brokenness will ever finally be healed, God says to us: "Jesus."

When we are not sure how to treat our friends, neighbors, and even enemies, God says to us: "Jesus."

Jesus, Jesus, Jesus ... it really is all about him. In John 1:1, the Bible calls Jesus the "Word" of God, which means that there is *never* a time when God is *not* declaring over the created order: "Jesus!" Never a time when he is not shouting over sinful humanity: "Jesus!" Never a time when he is not singing over the messy and confusing details of our lives: "Jesus!"

"Remember, our Message is not about *ourselves*," Paul wrote in 2 Corinthians 4:5; "we're proclaiming Jesus Christ, the Master. All we are is *messengers*, errand runners from Jesus to you" (emphasis added). Since "Jesus" is the Word of God, "Jesus" is also the "Word" of the church. And so we *sing* Jesus and *preach* Jesus and *pray* Jesus and *speak* Jesus to each other, knowing that as we do so, our identity becomes rooted more deeply in him, our lives are built more firmly upon him, and his glory and goodness shine ever brighter to the world around us.

. . .

Because God has made Jesus the Center of history, we strive to keep him the Center of our life as a community too. Here's how:

Jesus is at the center of our physical space.

As you approach New Life Church, you may notice that there is a cross on the top of our building. That's intentional. It is not a religious decoration, but rather a prophetic statement: We believe that what Jesus did for us on the cross stands tall over every human effort and achievement and that it speaks a word of forgiveness over every human misdeed and failure—reminders we desperately need.

Further, because Jesus said about his resurrection that when "I am lifted up from the earth, [I] will attract everyone to me and gather them around me" (John 12:32), we symbolically "lift him up" in anticipation of prodigals being called home. And yet the cross you see is far more than a symbol; it is a conviction, a way of life, and the essence both of *who* we are and of *whose* we are.

Jesus is at the center of the songs we sing.

Jesus also is at the center of the songs that we sing. Rather than drifting into music that simply mimics the *Billboard Top 100*, we fight hard around New Life to sing theologically sound, biblically rich worship songs that speak beautifully about the identity of God as Father, Son, and Holy Spirit and the great reconciling and redeeming work of Jesus, whose life, death, and resurrection have made a whole new way of living possible.

Paul, writing to the church at Ephesus, reminded the believers there to "to sing hymns instead of drinking songs! Sing songs from your heart to Christ. Sing praises over everything, any excuse for a song to God the Father in the name of our Master, Jesus Christ" (Ephesians 5:19). Our aim is to do just that.

Jesus is at the center of the message we preach.

You'll also notice that at New Life, the hero of every sermon we preach is the Messiah, Jesus, and that our teaching team makes a practice of preaching through books of the Bible. Since the Bible uniquely bears witness to Jesus, there is no better way to encounter him than to wrestle with biblical texts. In fact, Christian preaching is at its core the act of making Christ known through the Word of God. When one of our pastors gets up to preach, she or he knows that marriages are falling apart, that relationships are fracturing, that great hopes and dreams are hanging on by a thread, that people are struggling with addictions of various kinds, that many are lost and lonely and afraid, that countless souls are mired in condemnation and feelings of self-hatred, and that others are tangled up in bitterness and offense that is poisoning the well of their lives. What is more urgent for the pastor but to present Jesus in all his beauty and life-transforming power? Is there any other hope to be found?

Jesus left heaven to live among us. He healed bodies and instructed hearts. He died in our place, bearing the full weight of our sin. He rose triumphantly from the grave. We think that the best possible use of our pulpit, therefore, is to declare these great works of God's Son. "It's news I'm most proud to proclaim," Paul once wrote, "this extraordinary Message of God's powerful plan to rescue everyone who trusts him, starting with Jews and then right on to everyone else!" (Romans 1:16).

The news about what God has done for us in Jesus—the "gospel" is what it is called—*that news* is the real power of any preaching. If this gospel doesn't shine through in a sermon, then we think *a sermon hasn't been delivered at all.*

Jesus is at the head of the Table where we gather.

And then, finally, we believe that Jesus is to be at the head of "the Table," the Lord's Supper—*Communion* is what this sacrament is called.

The climactic moment in nearly all of our worship services is when we as a family—the rich and the poor, the young and the old, those who are both new to and mature in the faith—come to the Table of the Lord to receive the meal known as Communion.

On the night that Jesus went to his suffering and death on a cross, he instituted this meal. He gave thanks to the Father, broke bread, gave it to his disciples, and told them to eat it, saying, "This is my body." And then he took a cup of wine, gave thanks and blessed it, and gave it to them to drink, saying, "This is my blood, poured out for you."

The bread and the cup were symbols to the disciples of the work he was about to accomplish on the cross. But—and here's the critical thing—they were also *much more than symbols*. The word that the church has always used for them is "sacrament," which means a symbol that conveys the reality of what it represents. Somehow, Jesus himself comes to us at the Table, feeding us with his very life and providing himself as our All-Sufficient One once again. He blesses us and welcomes us, he strengthens us and enlivens us, he nourishes us and emboldens us for the work he would have us to do.

The ancient church used to call what happened at the Table a *communicatio idiomatum*—a communication of attributes. It believed that at the Table human brokenness was exchanged for Christ's wholeness, that our sin was exchanged for Christ's forgiveness, that death was exchanged for Christ's life.

That's our conviction, too. His life for ours—*The Great Exchange*. Which is why we hold fast to Jesus: the Center of it all.

CHAPTER 3

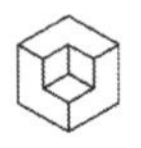

A GOSPEL FOR EVERYONE

Because of this decision we don't evaluate people by what they have or how they look. We looked at the Messiah that way once and got it all wrong, as you know. We certainly don't look at him that way anymore. Now we look inside, and what we see is that anyone united with the Messiah gets a fresh start, is created new. The old life is gone; a new life burgeons. Look at it! All this comes from the God who settled the relationship between us and him, and then called us to settle our relationships with each other. God put the world square with himself through the Messiah, giving the world a fresh start by offering forgiveness of sins.

God has given us the task of telling everyone what he is doing. We're Christ's representatives. God uses us to persuade men and women to drop their differences and enter into God's work of making things right between them. We're speaking for Christ himself now: Become friends with God; he's already a friend with you.

—2 CORINTHIANS 5.16-20

IF YOU WERE a Jewish person living in Jesus' day, then you would have had the world neatly divided into two groups of people: *us* and *them*. Indeed, 1st century Jewish life segregated people into the "chosen ones" and the "pagans." The chosen people, the nation of Israel, were the special objects of God's favor and affection; the pagans, on the other hand, were the Gentiles, the "nations" … quite simply, *sinners* … objects of God's disapproval.

For centuries, this is just how things went, with Jewish people in one corner and Gentiles in another—the original "tribalism," if you will. And then Jesus came.

Interestingly, when the news of Jesus' resurrection first hit the Mediterranean world, it was, first and foremost, a *Jewish* phenomenon—exclusively so. The New Testament book of Acts records that after Jesus' ascension, the disciples (who were Jewish, like Jesus), "were on their knees, worshiping him [Jesus]. They returned to Jerusalem bursting with joy. They spent all their time in the Temple praising God" (Luke 24:52-53).

For those first believers, what God had accomplished in Jesus was the fulfillment of their highest hopes and dreams *as Jewish people.* What the Law had pointed to, what the Prophets had foretold … *it had all come to pass in Jesus.* That's why they "spent all their time in the Temple praising God." They were giving thanks to the God of Abraham, Isaac, and Jacob for the way that he had, in Jesus, proven himself faithful to them.

And so, in the early period of the church, the gospel mainly circulated among Jews. Through the witness of those first believers, the God of Israel was reclaiming his people. A Jesus-shaped, Spirit-led, resurrection-fueled Jewish revival was underway. And the Jews—at least those who had responded to the Spirit's invitation—were *thrilled.*

Then one day the Holy Spirit led a God-fearing Gentile (read: *not a Jew*) named Cornelius to call for the apostle Peter, among others, to come to his house. Peter obliged, and when he arrived began to talk with the guests who were gathered there about the old barriers between Jews and Gentiles: "You know," Peter said, "I'm sure that this is highly irregular. Jews just don't do this—visit and relax with people of another race…" (Acts 10:28).

It wasn't the warmest of opening remarks, you might agree.

God decided to heat things up.

As Peter continued to talk, an amazing thing occurred. Verses 44 through 46 say this: "No sooner were these words out of Peter's mouth than the Holy Spirit came on the listeners. The believing Jews who had come with Peter couldn't believe it, couldn't believe that the gift of the Holy Spirit was poured out on 'outside' non-Jews, but there it was—they heard them speaking in tongues, heard them praising God."

This was a *radical* turn of events. But despite Peter's certain astonishment, through the preaching of the good news, God had broken through to these Gentile hearts and made them part of his kingdom movement. The only play left in Peter's playbook was to go along with it, to add his "amen" to God's "yes" over the worthiness of these Gentile lives: "Then Peter said, 'Do I hear any objections to baptizing these friends with water? They've received the Holy Spirit exactly as we did.'

"Hearing no objections, he [Peter] ordered that they be baptized in the name of Jesus Christ. Then they asked Peter to stay on for a few days" (vv. 47-48).

Then and there, the power of the resurrection overflowed its Jewish boundaries and began to spill into the Gentile world.

You might not realize it, but you and I are beneficiaries of what took place that day in Cornelius' house. The good news "broke out" beyond Jerusalem, Judea, and Samaria, and began to make its way to "the ends of the world" (Acts 1:8). This divine flow continues still today, renovating hearts and transforming lives, families, neighborhoods, and entire societies as it draws people into the single, united, Jew-plus-Gentile family known as "the church."

The gospel is for *everyone*. It was, it is, and it always will be.

. . .

At New Life, we believe that God's dream is that the life-transforming news of Jesus would touch the heart of every person on the planet, awakening faith. Paul wrote to his young protégé, Timothy, that God "wants not only us but *everyone* saved … everyone to get to know the truth *we've* learned: that there's one God and only one, and one Priest-Mediator between God and us—Jesus, who offered himself in exchange for everyone held captive by sin, to set them all free" (1 Timothy 2:4-5).

Everyone … did you catch that? *All* people, in *all* places, walking in God's truth. In other words, God doesn't have an us-versus-them mentality. He doesn't divide the world between those who "get it" and those who don't. He doesn't divide it between those who are "good" and those who aren't. He doesn't divide it between the especially religious and "enlightened" and those who may be less so.

He just doesn't see the world that way. And because of that, neither should we.

When God looks at the world, what he sees—regardless of our station in life or propensity for sin—is a beloved son, a beloved daughter, made in his image, worth the price of his beloved Son. Every human being who ever was, is, or will be *is worth Jesus*. In Jesus each of us is given inestimable dignity and honor. The heart of God burns with love for us all, and he is steadfast in his determination to call us home to that infinite love.

That God's love is "infinite" means that it is undivided. Think about it: Because God's love is infinite, he can and does tilt the whole of his fatherly affection toward each one of us, all the time. He can love one person with all that he is without diminishing or taking away from his love for another, or another, or another. As amazing as this may sound, we *all* are special objects of *all* of God's love, in *all* ways, *all* of the time. That's good news.

. . .

At New Life, we believe that the local church is to be a place where the "for everyone-ness" of the gospel can be seen. We want to be the kind of community where every*thing* we do and say speaks to every*one* in our midst, regardless of why they came or where they find themselves when they walked through our doors.

Every*thing* to every*one*—that's what we're shooting for. Further, we've found it helpful to think of three groups of people who, at any given time, are with us—whether on a Sunday morning or in our small groups or elsewhere. We want our messaging to fall to each of these groups, each with its distinctive questions and needs.

Ministering to the "Saints"

"Saints" are those who have said "yes"to Jesus, who have signed up for the Christian journey, and who are engaged in the gritty and glorious work of the kingdom with us. They are the disciples in our midst, fellow followers of Jesus Christ. The first "wave" of our messaging always addresses this group because the Bible prioritizes them. Read how Paul put it: "Get the word out. Teach all these things. And don't let anyone put you down because you're young. *Teach believers* with your life: by word, by demeanor, by love, by faith, by integrity. Stay at your post reading Scripture, giving counsel, teaching. And that special gift of ministry you were given when the leaders of the church laid hands on you and prayed—keep that dusted off and in use" (1 Timothy 4:11-13, emphasis added).

We "teach believers" first because we are exhorted in Scripture to teach believers first, to build up, strengthen, and equip the saints who are in our midst.

Now, to be sure, calling this group "the saints" is not meant to imply perfection—far from it—but rather an intent of the heart. These people have personally identified themselves with Jesus and his people and are committed to being perfected in Christ, transformed by his love and grace to transform the world around them. When this process of transformation is working as it should, it is beautiful to behold. Every week at New Life we hear stories of ordinary saints in our midst who by their kindness, love, and hospitality are drawing the lost to the love of Jesus. They are opening their homes and lives to people who do not yet know God. Through the graciousness of these faithful men and women, many who are "far off" are beginning to "taste and see that the Lord is good" (Psalm 34:8, NIV). And this is happening *through the saints*.

Women and men with questions about God and Jesus and the Bible and whether anything has any meaning at all are showing up at our gatherings *because ordinary New Lifers who love them are inviting them*. This is evangelism the way God intended. When our priority is on equipping the saints, helping them live ever-deeper in their Jesus-identity, the organic growth of the church is the natural result.

Ministering to the "Seekers and Cynics"

The second wave of our messaging is aimed at those we might call the seekers and the cynics, people who are seeking truth but have not yet grasped that Jesus is that truth they seek; people who often have hard and urgent questions about faith. John 14:6 says it this way: "Jesus said, 'I am the Road, also the Truth, also the Life. No one gets to the Father apart from me. If you really knew me, you would know my Father as well. From now on, you do know him. You've even seen him!'"

Seekers and cynics would like to believe in Jesus, but not yet. First, they need a few questions and concerns answered. In some cases, a *lot* of questions answered.

There's a brilliant scene recorded in the book of Acts that speaks to this. Paul has just finished preaching to a group of philosophically-minded Greek folks, telling them that their worship "to the god nobody knows" (Acts 17:23), might in fact be best understood as the worship of the God who raised Jesus from the dead. He declares to them that this God has "set a day when the entire human race will be judged and everything set right. And he has already appointed the judge, confirming him before everyone by raising him from the dead" (v. 31).

The writer of Acts concludes the story this way: "At the phrase, 'raising him from the dead,' the listeners split: Some laughed at him and walked off making jokes; others said, 'Let's do this again. We want to hear more" (v. 32). Apparently, Paul's words about the resurrection *provoked* something in these seekers. Some "sneered," of course. There will always be a few "sneer-ers" in our midst. The resurrection of Jesus from the dead is not a small thing to believe, after all, and many have a hard time accepting it. It's no surprise that many of them wander off after a little bit.

But others will be, and are, curious. They'll keep coming back, thinking, *"We want to hear more—we do."*

At New Life, we strive to make sure that our messaging speaks to those longing to hear more. We want it to *provoke* questions for the curious, the seekers, the cynics, the skeptics. At the same time, we want it to *challenge* how they view the world, not just *answering their questions*, but even, and maybe more importantly, *changing the questions they ask*. Admittedly, sometimes this commitment results in aggravation. We're not out to pick a fight, of course, but the good news about Jesus is *confrontative*, and that means that sometimes we'll make the seekers and cynics in our midst a bit angry. That's okay. We're not trying to be mean. We're just trying to tell about what we've seen in Jesus.

Still other times, and maybe more commonly, the aggravation will be from the "good church folk" in our midst. Our commitment to be a community that is radically welcoming to the seekers, cynics, and skeptics means that sometimes we'll find ourselves sitting next to people who smell like bourbon and cigarettes because they were out all night on Saturday.

On those occasions, well-meaning believers need to be reminded that *this is a very good thing*. While *membership* at New Life is contingent upon orthodox beliefs and a commitment to accountable, upright behavior, *hospitality* is not. Jesus said that his Father sent the warmth of the sun and cool of the rain to the nice and the nasty alike (Matthew 5:45). People who are accustomed to the local church being a religious country club or a museum for saints will be sorely disappointed with us, just as they were with Jesus in the 1st century. The religious people of Jesus' day often complained that he was a "friend of sinners," to which he often replied, "You'd better believe it."

He knew that the rough-and-tumble group around him needed him, and so he welcomed them with open arms, embracing all the odd smells, foul language, crass behavior, bizarre questions, and mountains of misunderstanding they brought. He knew of the Father's affection for them and modeled it without hesitation and without fail, receiving them in all their unfinished-ness.

And thus, so shall we.

Ministering to the "Prodigals"

There is another group in our midst each week: the prodigals, people who are just *away*. They've known the love of the Father. They've heard and believed the gospel of Jesus. They've tasted of the Holy Spirit. But for one reason or another, whether through their own choices or because of circumstances—usually it is a combination of the two—they've found themselves *away*—not experiencing the love of the Father, not sheltered and safe in genuine community.

The classic "prodigal" story in the Bible is found in Luke 15. A young man, loved and cherished by his father, decides to take his cut of his father's inheritance and bolt. He journeys into a far country and blows his money on wild living (see Luke 15:13). Broke, the son decides to hire himself out to a pig farmer. Penniless and starving, he comes to the point of *envying* the pigs: "He was so hungry he would have eaten the corncobs in the pig slop, but no one would give him any" (v. 16).

Eventually the son comes to his senses. His "aha" moment sounded like this: "'All those farmhands working for my father sit down to three meals a day, and here I am starving to death. I'm going back to my father. I'll say to him, "Father, I've sinned against God, I've sinned before you; I don't deserve to be called your son. Take me on as a hired hand." He got right up and went home to his father" (vv. 17-20).

The boy has come to a place of genuine brokenness, his old arrogance chiseled away by hard experience. So humbled is the young man that he's willing to forego his title and rights as a son *just in order to eat again* … It is all pain and hunger and humiliation and desperation for this young man. His self-talk drips with it.

Back to the groups in our midst at New Life. While the seekers and cynics are asking, "Are my questions safe here?" the prodigals are asking a far different question: *"Is it safe for me to confess my sins here?"*

Prodigals are aware of their brokenness and simply want to come home. They are aware of how much time and opportunity they've lost. They know what their failure has cost them and others. Their hearts hurt over it. The weight of their shame is crushing, the feelings of guilt suffocating. *They just want to come home.*

The best part is: God wants them to come home, too. Even worse than they want him, he wants them.

And, as a church, we also ache for them to come home. Again, from Luke 15: "When he [the son] was still a long way off, his father saw him. His heart pounding, he ran out, embraced him, and kissed him. The son started his speech: 'Father, I've sinned against God, I've sinned before you; I don't deserve to be called your son ever again.'

"But the father wasn't listening. He was calling to the servants, 'Quick. Bring a clean set of clothes and dress him. Put the family ring on his finger and sandals on his feet. Then get a grain-fed heifer and roast it. We're going to feast! We're going to have a wonderful time! My son is here—given up for dead and now alive! Given up for lost and now found!' And they began to have a wonderful time" (vv. 21-24).

The Father sees prodigals even when they are "a long way off," and just like the father in the story, God's heart swells with unabashed joy for them. He rushes to greet them. He brings out the best robe and the royal ring and fresh slippers and the finest steak and the best wine and throws a party to end all parties, because news of the return of one of his sons or daughters is the best news he could possibly receive.

And because *God* is like this, *we* are determined to be a community where it is safe for prodigals to let it all out, to name the ways that they've failed, and to know that because of what Jesus has done, they no longer have to live under a "fateful dilemma," as Romans 8:1 puts it, a "continuous, low-lying black cloud." When they walk through our doors with broken hearts, we want to fling the best robes over their shoulders as though they had never left.

Welcome home, son; welcome home, daughter... we're genuinely glad you're here.

This is why we work hard to make sure that we are *really* clear on how people can respond to Jesus each Sunday. True, we don't do a traditional "altar call" each week ... maybe you've noticed that. Instead, each time we gather as a family:

- We open the Scriptures;
- We let the Spirit present Jesus to us through them;
- We engage in a time of confession, opening our hearts to Jesus—
  wherever we are, whether saintly, cynical, or a bit prodigal; and then,
- We *come to the Table.*

Each week across our varied congregations, thousands of people rise from their seats and come forward to experience anew—and some for the first time—the love that makes royalty out of beggars. At the Table, the playing field is leveled. There is no spiritual hierarchy at the Table. At the Table, God makes "saints" out of us all—seekers, cynics, skeptics, prodigals—we all find ourselves named and loved and clothed with glory and honor.

What is required? Not a lot of spiritual gymnastics. Just saying "yes" to Jesus—that's all.

How is this possible? It's possible because the gospel of Jesus, the good news about the Father's healing, redeeming, life-creating, resurrecting love, *is for everyone*—saints, seekers, cynics, and prodigals alike.

CHAPTER 4

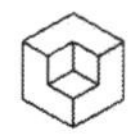

WHOLE-LIFE DISCIPLESHIP

The way God designed our bodies is a role model for understanding our lives together as a church: every part dependent on every other part, the parts we mention and the parts we don't, the parts we see and the parts we don't. If one part hurts, every other part is involved in the hurt, and in the healing. If one part flourishes, every other part enters into the exuberance.

You are Christ's body—that's who you are! You must never forget this. Only as you accept your part of that body does your "part" mean anything.

—1 CORINTHIANS 12.25-27

SOME TWO THOUSAND years ago, while walking one day along the lush landscape surrounding the Sea of Galilee, Jesus noticed two brothers, Simon Peter and Andrew, casting their nets into the lake. The brothers were fishermen. And not in a "weekend warrior" sense, either; for Simon Peter and Andrew, fishing was their trade, their occupation. It was what they *did* that earned a living and contributed to the world.

While we aren't explicitly told this about the brothers' work, knowing what we know about 1st century life, it is almost certain that fishing was the family business. Dad did it. And granddad before him. And probably great-granddad before him, a robust "family economy" passed down from generation to generation. So, fishing wasn't just about *money* for the brothers; it was about *place* and *identity* and *purpose* and *belonging*—so much more than mere income. *This is who you are, and this is what you do: you fish. You're a fisherman, just like us.*

It is hard for the modern mind to conceive of such a world in which family, identity, task, and future are bound so tightly together, in which the script of your life is written for you before you were born. Our rugged individualism makes it almost impossible for us to see, much less to appreciate, how human history up until very recently has been defined by this kind of arrangement. But so it has been. In fact, if you look closely, you can still see vestiges of this kind of a world in our culture today. Surnames like *Smith* and *Miller*, *Abbot* and *Baker, Carver* and *Cook,* and *Porter* and *Potter* originally were designated not just for *family identity* but for *family task and occupation*.

If you were born into the "Smith" family, you had a share in the work of "smith-ing," according to your gifts and abilities. If you were born into the "Miller" family, you had a share in the work of "milling," according to your gifts and abilities. If you were born into the, "Zuckerman" family, you had a share in the work of "zuckerman-ing," according to your gifts and abilities. (In case the suspense is too tough to bear, a "zuckerman" was a sugar merchant.) Identity, belonging, and task—all part of a seamless garment. And into that situation, the Messiah shouts: "Come with me. I'll make a new kind of fisherman out of you. I'll show you how to catch men and women instead of perch and bass" (Matthew 4:19).

With this context in mind, it's easier to appreciate what Jesus was doing. He wasn't just asking these career fishermen if they'd like to join him on a little short-term mission trip. Instead, he was calling them to leave behind an old life to find identity, belonging, and purpose in a new life with him. And notice this: He doesn't *ask*, "Hey guys, I have a really great opportunity for you that you may want to consider." No, he *commands*. He *summons*. Shockingly, they did as they were told. "They didn't ask questions," verse 20 says, "but simply dropped their nets and followed."

No questions asked? For real?

Upon hearing the Master's call, these men were so compelled to do as he said that they quite literally left behind their life and their existence to find new purpose, new identity in him.

As if to drive the point home, Matthew then includes this detail: "A short distance down the beach they came upon another pair of brothers, James and

John, Zebedee's sons. These two were sitting in a boat with their father, Zebedee, mending their fishnets. Jesus made the same offer to them, and they were just as quick to follow, abandoning boat and father" (vv. 21-22).

Again, no questions asked. Just immediate followership. And just like that, in the span of a few moments, the first community of Jesus was born: Jesus, Simon Peter and Andrew, James and John. *Bye, Mom and Dad. See ya later. We've found a new family, and there's new work for us to do ...*

. . .

Saying "yes" to Jesus' call to "follow me" was a pretty radical thing, you might agree. But the trade-off was equally weighty—for the first disciples then, and for us today. For by saying "yes" to Jesus, we say "yes" to greater belonging, greater purpose, and greater impact here on earth. When we say "yes" to Jesus, we say "yes" to becoming sharers in his ongoing ministry through the people who bear his name. We say "yes" to divine power. "Yes," to supernatural insight. "Yes," to spiritual fruit such as joy and peace. "Yes," to the "life that is truly life," as 1 Timothy 6:19 calls it, together with his people. What it meant to be a disciple in the 1st century is what it means to be a disciple in our here-and-now world: leaving everything behind for the sake of finding ourselves in the company of Christ and his people.

As you'd expect, our approach to ministry at New Life centers on this theme. We believe that a big part of our mission is to help others to say "yes" to

Jesus, to become caught up in his family of followers, to enjoy a share in his ongoing work, and to experience life that is truly life.

We're calling people, in other words, into *whole-life discipleship* with us.

Christ calls each one of us to find belonging among his people, where rich sit next to poor, where old sit next to young, where healthy sit next to infirm. This is an essential mark of the church—to be a place where each of us lends and receives just what we need, each as we are able, so that the overall community is vibrant and strong.

At New Life, we're fighting hard to develop a church family where we see ourselves and one another as *partners in the ongoing ministry of Jesus* rather than *consumers of religious goods and services*. We understand how lonely and isolating the world can be, and so, instead of adding to the loneliness and isolation by promoting an "anonymous" form of Christianity, *we're doing the opposite*: We're trying to make New Life church the hardest church in the world for people to remain unknown. We want every person who walks through our doors to know how glad we are to have them with us, and how eager we are to help them find their place in our family. We want them to know it in their bones, on a *cellular* level. We want the sweet aroma of hospitality to be *everywhere*. That's why simple kindness is vitally important to us. Paul says in Romans 2:4 that it is God's *kindness* that leads us to repentance. Kindness awakens something in us. It draws us *in* and keeps drawing us *back*—back to the source for more, to the Source behind the source, which is Jesus himself.

Whether you're aware of it or not, all of us on some level are in the family of God because someone was *kind* to us, because they showed us *hospitality*. They were open-hearted and "open-lifed" to us. They met us in our questions, shared Jesus with us, created space at the table for us, and watched the Spirit work. Without hospitality, without kindness, true conversion never occurs.

Hospitality is modeling the infinite welcome of God to other people. The local church is to be a family that models God's hospitable presence, the openness of his own life, in everything we do. When we do this, we discover, time and again, that people are reconciled to God, finding belonging and purpose among his people.

We see it every week in our community. One Friday night a man wandered into one of our services right off the street. He'd been through a season that was personally and professionally devastating; and though he'd never really been to church before, he decided on this night to give it a try. The Spirit rushed over him through the worship and the words of the sermon. He sat in the back with his head in his hands and wept.

At the end of the service, he filled out a guest card. One of our pastors called him that week, listened to him pour his heart out for a half an hour, prayed for him, and invited him to meet for dinner at the church the following week. The man did. And once again, he wept through the service. He remarked afterward, "I haven't cried like this in years. I don't really know what's going on in me, but I know it's good, and I know this is where I need to be."

We happen to feel the same way. It was kindness that first compelled us to draw near to Christ, and it will be kindness that compels others to similarly draw near.

Kindness, hospitality, openheartedness—these things are the very fragrance of Christ wafting out from the people of God to a world that is lonely, disheartened, and afraid. Through them God situates people in his family, giving them new meaning, identity, and purpose.

Doing community this way is deeply biblical. It is also, at times, deeply messy. Real community requires that we open our hearts and lives to those who are works in progress at best. In fact, some *aren't even on the assembly line yet*. Remember, there are plenty of seekers, cynics, and skeptics in our midst who need some time before they start taking more concrete steps towards Jesus. Still, we're confident—by conviction and experience—that the Holy Spirit is at work in our connections with each other, making friends of strangers, family members of orphans, disciples of rebels. Our job is simply to crack open the goodness and warmth of our community's life to people, and watch God do his good work.

. . .

Some time ago, the way that many church leaders thought about community and the disciple-making process followed this type of progression:

Believe → Belong → Become

First, a person needed to believe the right things. They needed to say the sinner's prayer and sign a doctrinal statement on the dotted line, which allowed them to have a seat at the table, a place in the family —"membership," it was called. Through that process, they would eventually "become" all that God desired them to be.

At face value this approach makes sense. These churches strived to preserve a form of doctrinal and behavioral purity, which is a laudable goal indeed. But the progression we believe Jesus endorsed has those first two steps reversed. At New Life, this is how community unfolds:

Belong → Believe → Become

Jesus' disciples, as we've seen, didn't know much about him at all before they started following him. There was just something about his personality and the command of his voice that compelled them to come, and so they did. In the process, he revealed himself to them in greater depth and complexity. In that journey of *belonging-and-believing*, they found their lives changed. They *became.*

That's exactly what we work to do. It is for this reason that when homeless families or single moms or people in any kind of need wander into our community, we help them. We give them what we can. We wash their feet and serve them. And we do it all without any strings attached. Because that's the way that Jesus did it. We set the table, remember? And God? He does the rest.

To drill down further into how this belong-believe-become progression works in our midst, you'll find that we often refer to a pattern of doing life together using these three words: *worship*, *connect*, and *serve.*

We experience life together through worship.

At the center of the community of faith's life together are its regular patterns of *worship*. Worship is what makes us who we are. Because we worship the God who has revealed himself as Father, Son, and Holy Spirit, we are marked apart from the world in important ways. When we gather for worship, the Spirit takes our messy lives and conforms them to the Son through whom we rise to the Father in full-hearted obedience.

Something happens when we gather for worship. We're reminded of who we are. We're called anew by the Father. We're blessed by the Son. We're filled with the Holy Spirit. Some theologians would say that when we gather for worship, we are "re-constituted" as Christ's people. Another way of saying that would be to say that we are "re-membered" as Christ's body—the members of the body, separated during the week, visibly come together again in praise to the Father, through the Son, by the Holy Spirit.

In worship we are given a picture of where the world is headed. The book of Revelation envisions a day in which multitudes of people are gathered up before the throne of God, crying out, "*Holy, holy, holy* ..." Each Sunday our gathered worship is a visible reminder, a signpost, of where the heavens and the earth and all that is in them are headed: *full-throated doxology*. When we gather for worship and Christ is exalted in our midst, the kingdom shines through.

But there is more. Gathering for worship has a way of resetting the meter and rebooting our own personal lives of worship and devotion. We are *each* called to this, in personal and private ways. Jesus talked about praying in secret (see Matthew 6:6), where we are seen and known and loved by our Father. Paul encouraged the individuals in his churches to pray continuously (see 1 Thessalonians 5:17). Corporate worship reminds us that God desires for us to carry the flame of worship and prayer into our homes, businesses, and neighborhoods so that he can flood the world with his glory.

We experience life together through connection.

As we've said throughout this book, the life of faith is inescapably communal and corporate. *Connecting with each other* in deep and meaningful ways, therefore, is a core part of what we mean at New Life when we say, "We follow Jesus." Because Jesus calls us to a rich, shared life together, we're constantly seeking ways to open our lives more profoundly to each other.

One of the stereotypes people often have of large churches like ours is that because they are big, they are also difficult to connect with. In fact, the most common reason we hear from people on why they didn't want to come to New Life (until they actually came, of course) is simply, "It's too big." The implication is, "*… and I won't be able to connect there.*"

We've worked hard and continue to work hard to be what we've sometimes called "the smallest big church in America." What we mean by that is that we're constantly developing layer upon layer of rich and meaningful community, easy "onramps" for people to find their place among us, and a welcoming, hospitable atmosphere where no one who walks into our congregations needs to feel like a stranger.

You wouldn't believe how God has worked through these efforts. Community, we've found, is a miracle through which God brings continuing miracles. Every week we hear stories of people who were lost, wayward, hurt, isolated, lonely, and confused, who wandered into our community, connected with other New Lifers, and found their lives utterly transformed by it.

In the same way that we experience the Person of Christ through the bread and the cup when we come to the Table of the Lord ("This is my body, this is my blood," said Jesus), so too we experience the Person of Christ by allowing our lives to be incorporated into his body, the local church. Just like our own spirits animate our bodies with life, so the Spirit of God animates the body of Christ with the very life of God, a life that courses through us as we are incorporated into the body and heals us. That's the power of the community known as "the church."

We experience life together through service.

We believe that the word "serve" names the many ways that we are called to use what God has given us for the good of others—both in the community of faith and beyond it. And he has given us much, regardless of our religious background or station in life.

Our gifts, talents, resources, experiences, personalities, and "spiritual gifts"—the Spirit-inspired abilities that the New Testament talks about, such as the gifts of healing and miracles, discernment and prophecy, preaching and teaching and more, which are intended for the building up of the body of Christ—can be employed to bless those beyond the walls of the church. God desires to see each of us to put what he's given us to use, serving others with all that we are.

When you walk around any of our congregations, you'll notice lots of people, busy as bees, serving others. Most of them are unpaid. Thousands of people volunteer with us on a regular basis. They do that because they believe that's what it means to follow Jesus. With him, remember, we're given both *a place of belonging* and also *a share in his ministry.*

And that ministry spills out beyond our walls to the city around us. We have a saying around here: *"We're in the city for the sake of the city."* That's a core conviction of ours. It's why we partner with homeless shelters and prisons; it's why we've started a free women's clinic and a transitional housing program for single moms; it's why our pastors spend time with city officials, learning how we can be a bigger blessing to Colorado Springs. This is part of the essence of who we are … we are here to serve.

We believe that our life belongs to Jesus. And because it belongs to Jesus, it belongs to *those he came to save.*

In worship, we give our lives away to him again.

In connection, he gives us to each other afresh.

In service, we give ourselves away to one another and to the world he loves as one body, united by faith.

CHAPTER 5

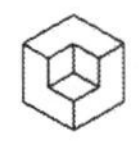

GROUNDED IN A BIGGER STORY

The first thing I did was place before you what was placed so emphatically before me: that the Messiah died for our sins, exactly as Scripture tells it; that he was buried; that he was raised from death on the third day, again exactly as Scripture says ...

—1 CORINTHIANS 15.3-4

WE TEND TO associate the image of a lighthouse with a picturesque view from a pier in a quaint vacation locale. Lighthouses to most of us are charming, serene, even *cute*. For sailors living before the rise of modern electronic navigational systems, however, the lighthouse was *anything but*. It was, truth be told, a matter of life and death. Lighthouses served as an important guide to maritime pilots, helping them steer clear of dangerous shorelines, reefs, or rugged outcroppings of rock that would rip the vessel to pieces. By heeding the lighthouse, travelers were able to maintain a sense of direction in a disorienting environment, finding their way to their desired destination. Without them—and other navigational guides, both natural and man-made—the journey was likely doomed to failure.

Similarly, in the old prairie days, farmers used to take a rope and connect it from the house to the barn so that in blizzard or whiteout conditions they'd be able to find their way home when the day's chores were done. Without the rope, the farmer's sense of direction was easily lost—often, tragically, their lives right along with it.

The rope, like the lighthouse, was a matter of life and death.

As followers of Jesus living in the 21st century, we too face treacherous conditions from time to time, causing us confusion, frustration, and angst. We too can become disoriented, running the risk of losing our way. We too need a light or a lifeline that can help us get back home.

We think that light, that lifeline is, quite simply, God's Word as it is contained in the Old and New Testaments: the Bible.

. . .

But what is the Bible? Some say that the Bible is a book of spiritual wisdom and pithy sayings to help us get through life. Some say that it is a rulebook, teaching us what to do and what to avoid. Still others say that the Bible is a book of prophecy concerning the end of the world.

To all of that we would say—yes, yes, and yes. But that's not all, or even primarily, what it is. The Bible, before it is anything else, is a story—a narrative unlike any narrative you will ever read.

The Bible, according to its own witness, is not just *a* story among other stories in our world, but rather is *The Story* that gives meaning to all other stories. It is the *ultimate* story—about love and loss and new life, about wandering off and coming home, about the heroic quest to save someone or something from calamity. The Bible is the story—the drama—of how God is with us, for our good, forever, despite everything.

Let's look at what, exactly, that grand story is about.

A Play in Four Acts

It's not uncommon for theologians to speak of the Bible as a "play" comprising several major "acts." Along these lines, those acts might look something like this:

Act 1 : Creation
Act 2 : The Fall
Act 3 : Resurrection
Act 4 : The New Creation

Let's look at each in turn.

Act 1: Creation

According to Moses' account in the book of Genesis, God created the heavens and the earth—everything we see—in an act of boundless love, freedom, and joy. The stars and skies and seas; every proton, neutron, atom, and quark; the forests and the fields; mountains high and valleys low; birds and fish and furry little critters—all of it was spun into being by the Creator God, designed to reflect his glory.

The crown of God's creative work was *humanity;* human beings are made, Genesis 1:26-27 says, "in the image of God"; they are given the power to love, reason, and make choices; and they are invited to share with God in his wise, loving rule over the earth.

Act 2: The Fall

All was well in creation until humankind believed Satan's lies. Genesis 3 recounts the day when Adam and Eve, the earth's first couple, rejected God by choosing to go their own way. "The Fall" is what this is commonly called, and the results have been disastrous.

Because Eve and then Adam did the very thing God instructed them not to do—eat of the fruit from the Tree of the Knowledge of Good and Evil—a curse fell upon God's good creation, bringing war and plague, famine and flood, violence and hatred and strife onto the otherwise glorious scene. Of this tragic turn of events, the apostle Paul later would write that “the wages of sin is death” (Romans 6:23). To be sure, whenever our connection is broken to Life himself—our Heavenly Father—death is the inevitable result.

“Death,” then, is the name of what we see all around us—in broken homes and broken marriages, in broken spirits and broken minds, in urban decay and the neglect of the poor, in abuse of power and racism’s awful ways. Because of sin, the plague of death is everywhere, slumping our shoulders and crushing our souls.

Truly, this is where the story would have ended, were it not for God’s intervening grace.

Act 3: Redemption

Despite humankind’s deviance, the Genesis account further teaches that God refused to let failure have the last word. Immediately after the Fall, God enacted his rescue plan by calling a man named Abraham to become the father of many nations. “Leave your country, your family, and your father’s home for a land that I will show you,” God told Abraham, as recorded in Genesis 12:1-3. “I’ll make you a great nation and bless you. I’ll make you famous; you’ll be a blessing. I’ll bless those who bless you; those who curse you I’ll curse. All the families of the Earth will be blessed through you.” *Blessing* would touch and restore all that had been cursed by the Fall.

God proves faithful to keeping his promise, even as Abraham’s family—the nation Israel—repeatedly turns from God. The testimony of the Old Testament is God saying, in essence, “Even though you won’t keep your commitment to me, I will keep mine to you. And through your flawed participation, I will bless the entire world."

When the time was right, God, through the lineage of Abraham, sent his Son, Jesus, into the world. The gospels of Matthew, Mark, Luke, and John confirm that Jesus took on a human body like yours and mine; that he suffered the full consequences of our sin in his body on a Roman cross; and that, three days later, he rose to new life again, triumphant over Satan, sin, and death.

The death and resurrection of Jesus is God's great, victorious answer to the Fall. And now, by God's Spirit, John 6:44 tells us that God is drawing people to himself to find their lives made whole in him, to become part of what the apostle Paul called "a new kind of human being" (Ephesians 2:15), those who serve one another and the world around them in love, always reaching out to wayward sons and daughters to bring them home. These people, of course, form the "body of Christ," the co-heirs of God's glory, the church.

Act 4: New Creation

The news gets better still, for one day the work that God began when he raised Jesus from the dead will find its completion in what John in the book of Revelation calls "Heaven and earth—new created" (Revelation 21:1).

The ensuing passage reads:

> *I heard a voice thunder from the Throne: "Look! Look! God has moved into the neighborhood, making his home with men and women! They're his people, he's their God. He'll wipe every tear from their eyes. Death is gone for good—tears gone, crying gone, pain gone—all the first order of things gone." The Enthroned continued, "Look! I'm making everything new. Write it all down—each word dependable and accurate (Revelation 21:3-5).*

"Everything new"—that is where our story is headed, which is why in Colossians 1:18 Jesus is referred to as the "firstborn from among the dead," (NIV). His death and resurrection have made the great renewal that God promises at the end of all things possible. He is the first glimpse of where God is taking his good-yet-broken creation, and those who put their faith in him have a share in his resurrected, "new creation" life. One day we'll live forever with him, our conquering King, in the new heavens and the new earth.

A Story-Formed People

Based on these major "acts," it's not a leap to regard the people of God as a "story-formed" people. Everything that we *do*, everything that we *are*, is based on what God has done—in creation, in redemption, in restoration—and who he has shown himself to be, both for us and for the world he loves. We're part of this *bigger story*, this rescue plan that was imagined from the start. We're part of *God's* story. We are sharers in its blessing, carriers of its benefit to the world around us. This is true for us today just like it was true of God's people long ago. We are a story-formed people, which is why the nation Israel framed the patterns of their worship around the memory of God's faithfulness, his mighty deeds.

We find a powerful illustration of this reality in the book of Deuteronomy. Moses, the great leader of Israel, knows that his end is near. The people are barely a generation removed from their miraculous deliverance from Egypt known as "the exodus" and are preparing to enter into the Promised Land—the land God had sworn to their forefathers to give them. This was a land that was free of oppression … a land to call their own. Moses imagines a tender exchange between parent and child upon their arrival to this longed-for land:

> *The next time your child asks you, "What do these requirements and regulations and rules that GOD, our God, has commanded mean?" (Deuteronomy 6:20)*

In response, Moses advises the parent to give the following explanation:

> *[T]ell your child, "We were slaves to Pharaoh in Egypt and God powerfully intervened and got us out of that country. We stood there and watched as God delivered miracle-signs, great wonders, and evil-visitations on Egypt, on Pharaoh and his household. He pulled us out of there so he could bring us here and give us the land he so solemnly promised to our ancestors. That's why God commanded us to follow all these rules, so that we would live reverently before God, our God, as he gives us this good life, keeping us alive for a long time to come. It will be a set-right and put-together life for us if we make sure that we do this entire commandment in the Presence of God, our God, just as he commanded us to do" (Deuteronomy 6:20-25).*

To the question, "Why do we do what we do?" Moses proposes an answer: *Once upon a time* ... In other words: *Tell them a story*. When your kids become curious about who we are and why we do what we do, how we wound up in this land at all, *tell them a story*.

Tell them about how we were slaves in Egypt. Tell them about how our cry went up before the Lord and he heard our voice. Tell them that he delivered us with a mighty hand and an outstretched arm. Tell them about how all of this was done in faithfulness to promises that God made to our ancestors, to Abraham, Isaac, and Jacob. Tell them that we do these things because this is who we are based on what God has done for us. And tell them that they are part of the ongoing story of how God is with us for our good forever.

When you're looking for something to tell them, please, *tell them a story*. Tell them my story. Tell them *the* story, the story on which all other stories are based.

. . .

The ancient church had many "maxims"—sayings that summarized large truths. One of their most profound was this: *lex orandi, lex credendi, lex vivendi*.

The maxim meant that how you pray and worship *(lex orandi),* how you believe *(lex credenda),* and how you live *(lex vivendi)* are all interconnected aspects of the same reality, impossible to strip apart. The people of Israel knew that by "encoding" the memory of God's mighty deeds into the patterns of their worship, they would be able to maintain a sense of direction, identity, and purpose amid the changing circumstances of their lives. Those memories would remind them of who—and whose—they were.

It is the same today. A story has a way of doing that. Think of the times when you've sat around the table with your family or close friends. Besides catching up on current events, the conversations that unfold usually center on the stories of who you are. Stories of shared past experiences. Stories of dreams and goals. Stories of hardships overcome. Stories of foibles and missteps and pain. Often these are stories you all know by heart and have heard or told a thousand times before, but still you savor their *re*-telling. Why? Because sharing those stories reinforces the "we" and creates energy for future relationship. *That's* the power of a shared story.

Similarly, as followers of Jesus in this day and age, we are a people formed by the story of what God—Father, Son, and Holy Spirit—has done, is doing, and will do in the world. The story is our lighthouse, our rope back to the barn. In a world that is doing everything it can to strip us of our identity, or to convince us that the only valid identity we can have is the one we create for ourselves, the story of the Bible reminds us of who we are and why we exist. It tethers us to the eternal, the unchanging, the realest reality we know.

In one of the earliest letters on record, the apostle Paul wrote to the Corinthian church these words: "The first thing I did was place before you what was placed so emphatically before me: that the Messiah died for our sins, exactly as Scripture tells it; that he was buried; that he was raised from death on the third day, again exactly as Scripture says" (1 Corinthians 15:3-4). The gospel was not a plotline Paul wrote on the fly; no, it was *given* to him for him to faithfully expand upon and hand on to others. It was centered on Jesus—his death, burial, and resurrection—and was "exactly as Scripture tells it," which is a way of saying that it brought the great Old Testament story to its climax.

Much of the effort of Paul's ministry was to say to communities of believers who were under constant pressure to be led astray by false gospels, or who suffered occasional fits of "spiritual amnesia": "*Don't forget who you are and whose story you're living in. Don't forget that the texture of the universe is shaped by Father, Son, and Holy Spirit. Don't forget that Christ has died, Christ is risen, and that Christ will come again. Don't forget that you are his unique people, bought with his own blood, filled with his Spirit, called for his purposes.*"

In other words: "You are the family of God. Don't forget that this is your story!"

At New Life, we believe that we've likewise been given something indescribably precious; that we are to be carriers of a great deposit of beauty, meaning, and truth; and that we are to prove ourselves faithful in stewarding this great, "once, upon a time" story.

Grounded in the Story

So, how do we stay true to this mission? How do we keep ourselves grounded in the grand story of God? There are two important practices that help us with this: the Creed and the Table of the Lord.

The Creed

One observation you may make upon visiting our church is that our official "statement of faith" is, well, a little *odd*, at least for a large non-denominational church like ours. It goes like this:

We believe in one God,
the Father, the Almighty,
Maker of heaven and earth,
of all that is, seen and unseen.

We believe in one Lord, Jesus Christ,
the only Son of God,
Eternally begotten of the Father,
God from God, Light from Light,
True God from true God,
begotten, not made,
of one Being with the Father.
Through him all things were made.
For us and for our salvation
he came down from heaven:
By the power of the Holy Spirit
he became incarnate from the Virgin Mary
And was made man.
For our sake he was crucified under Pontius Pilate;
He suffered death and was buried.
On the third day he rose again
in accordance with the Scriptures;
He ascended into heaven
and is seated at the right hand of the Father.
He will come again in glory to judge the living and the dead,
And his kingdom will have no end.

We believe in the Holy Spirit, the Lord, the giver of life,
Who proceeds from the Father [and the Son][6].
With the Father and the Son he is worshiped and glorified.
He has spoken through the Prophets.
We believe in one holy catholic[7] and apostolic Church.
We acknowledge one baptism for the forgiveness of sins.
We look for the resurrection of the dead,
And the life of the world to come.
Amen.

---

[6] The earliest versions of the Nicene Creed do not contain the words "and the Son."

[7] The word "catholic" here means "universal"; it is not a reference to the Roman Catholic Church.

Sound familiar? If so, it is because our statement of faith is simply the words of the Nicene Creed, one of the oldest and most widely accepted summations of the Christian faith. The Nicene Creed dates back to the 4th century, when a large group of church leaders assembled to clarify the central doctrines of Christianity. Amid the changes the global church has seen in the centuries which have followed its drafting, the Creed has—quite remarkably—stood the test of time. Christians from every stream of the body of Christ can and do confess these words: Catholic, Protestant, Eastern Orthodox, Lutheran, Reformed, Presbyterian, Baptist, Pentecostal, and more. Each of these groups would say of the Creed: *This, we believe*. What a gift!

It is important to understand, however, that the Nicene Creed is not simply an intellectual checklist of doctrine. Rather, the Creed is a confession of worship that forms us as the people of God and draws us together into the very life of the Father, Son, and Holy Spirit. This is why the stanzas of the Creed begin not with "We *think* that," or "We *feel* that," or even "We *believe* that …" No, the Creed declares: "We *believe in* …" and then names the Name and the work of each member of the Godhead in the plan of salvation. The Nicene Creed is a bold declaration of the God in whom the church has put all her trust. And it is a statement that *we do in fact trust him now.* "*We believe …*"

You'll notice as well that there is a *narrative* pattern to the Creed: it begins with Creation (first stanza); it moves from Creation to Redemption (second stanza); and it concludes with the shift from Redemption to New Creation (third stanza). The Nicene Creed, in other words, is a story. *The* Story, as a matter of fact. When we say the word "doctrine," what we're really talking about is *how do we tell the Story right?* The Creed helps us tell our story the right way. "First say this, then this, then this …"—this is how the story goes. The stanzas of the Creed are the main lines of the "plot," and its primary characters are:

- the Father, the maker and creator, whose own life is the fountainhead of all things, seen and unseen (first stanza);
- the Son, eternally begotten of the Father, incarnate of the Virgin Mary, redeemer of the world (second stanza);
- the Spirit, who proceeds from the Father and the Son, giving life and bearing witness to the great work of God (third stanza).

You might have noticed that the church, as a character, also has a place in the Creed. Tucked into the stanza on the Holy Spirit are the words, "*We believe in one, holy, catholic* (some versions say "universal")*, and apostolic Church* ..." The Church is not equal to God, or to any member of the godhead. She is, instead, *the direct result of God being the God he is to the world.*

So, when we gather for worship and take the words of the Nicene Creed on our lips (as we do regularly), we are reminded …

of the Father who made us,
and of the Son who redeemed us,
and of the Spirit who breathes upon us

to wake us up to resurrection life, healing us, making us witnesses of the coming kingdom of God. It is in *this God* that we've placed all our trust.

In the end, the Creed reminds us that our individual stories find their grounding in God's bigger, grander story. That our lives are wrapped up in his life. And despite the many ways the world around us screams otherwise, the Creed declares boldly that the world we live in is not headed for final collapse and meaninglessness but for final renewal in the everlasting kingdom of God. The Creed reminds us that we, the people of God, are a people of *hope*, or we are nothing, and that our hope is "built on nothing less" (as the old hymn "On Christ the Solid Rock" puts it), than on God himself and what he has accomplished for us in Christ. Further, the Creed reminds us that this hope is not the possession of one or another *group* of Christians, but rather it is the inheritance of all of those who call on Christ as Lord.

Admittedly, the Nicene Creed neither answers all of our questions nor settles all of our disputes. Truth be told, it wasn't designed to do that. The Creed leaves room for a lot of debate and wrestling and *mystery,* and we think that's a good thing. What the Creed *does* do, however, is beautifully bind us to the historical and global Church. It sets forth the main lines of the plot and the main characters in the story. And it reminds us of who we are and whose we are and where this whole cosmic tale is headed.

The Table

As we noted in Chapter 2, the great crescendo of all of our worship services is the moment when we come, broken and empty-handed, to the Table of the Lord, to Communion. This coming together of Jesus and his people, where he meets personally with us, communicating his life into our weary souls and bodies, is another great historic practice we honor at New Life to keep us grounded in God's bigger tale.

Though many Christians today do not realize it, historians agree that when the early church gathered for worship, the climax of their times together was the celebratory meal of remembrance and thanksgiving known as Communion. Alternatively called "The Lord's Supper," "The Lord's Table," or "The Eucharist" (a Greek word meaning "thanksgiving"), the meal called to mind the night that Jesus was handed over to suffering and death, where he took bread, gave thanks to his Father, broke it, gave it to his disciples and said:

> *Take, eat.*
> *This is my body.*

Likewise, he took a cup of wine, gave thanks, drank from it, and gave it to his disciples saying,

> *Drink this, all of you.*
> *This is my blood, God's new covenant poured out for many people for the forgiveness of sins.*

For the early church, the communion meal was a *memorial*, a place of *remembrance* that anchored them anew in the Story. It preached the death of Christ and announced that he would come again. "I tell you," Jesus said, "I'll not be drinking wine from this cup again until that new day when I'll drink with you in the kingdom of my Father" (Matthew 26:29).

So, the meal pointed *backward* in remembrance but also *forward* in hope—that the One who was crucified, Jesus, was also *raised* and would, as the Creed declares, "return again in glory" to usher in the kingdom.

But the meal did more than that. The early church believed that Christ Jesus was personally present at the Table. Jesus didn't say of the bread, "This is *kind of like* my body," or of the cup, "This is *kind of like* my blood"; but "This *is* my body" and "This *is* my blood." Leaders of the church, like the apostle Paul, took these words of Jesus seriously, as evidenced by Paul's assessment in 1 Corinthians 10:

> *When we drink the cup of blessing, aren't we taking into ourselves the blood, the very life, of Christ? And isn't it the same with the loaf of bread we break and eat? Don't we take into ourselves the body, the very life of Christ? Because there is one loaf, our many-ness becomes one-ness—Christ doesn't become fragmented in us. Rather, we become unified in him. We don't reduce Christ to what we are; he raises us to what he is (vv. 16-17).*

Subsequent generations of Jesus-followers have had some pretty heated debates about what *precisely* Paul—and Jesus, before him—meant when they made these statements. But this much, we believe, is clear: Jesus has pledged to meet us *truly* and *personally* at the Table.

So, the Table of the Lord is not just a place of remembrance and hope, but also a place of *encounter*. The past, the present, and the future rush together when we gather at the Table. At New Life, we like to say it like this: "Communion is the bridge between a miraculous, resurrected past, a hopeful present, and a prophetic future."

Moreover, because we believe that it is *Christ himself* whom we meet at the Table, and because Christ is never without his body, the Church, coming to the Table connects us as a single, local expression of the body of Christ to the great wide church universal, to the global and historical communion of saints. And it gives us a space in a story, God's story, that was already being written long before our lives began.

. . .

Interestingly, when we read about the second coming of Christ in the book of Revelation, we see that a *meal* plays a central role. Here is what the writer, John, had to say:

> *Then I heard the sound of massed choirs, the sound of a mighty cataract, the sound of strong thunder:*
>
> *Hallelujah! The Master reigns, our God, the Sovereign-Strong! Let us celebrate, let us rejoice, let us give him the glory! The Marriage of the Lamb has come; his Wife has made herself ready. She was given a bridal gown of bright and shining linen. The linen is the righteousness of the saints. The Angel said to me, "Write this: 'Blessed are those invited to the Wedding Supper of the Lamb.'" He added, "These are the true words of God!" (Revelation19:6-9)*

Because of this scene, we can say with certainty that whenever we gather around the Lord's Table, we're experiencing in the present the future that God has planned for us. Communion is a picture of where we are headed with God, where the heavens and the earth are careening, by the power of the Spirit—to a place where there is no more death, or mourning, or sorrow, or decay; to the replacement of the old order of things by the new; to us-with-God: Father, Son, and Holy Spirit; to music and singing and dancing. *Lots* of dancing, we dare say.

To something a lot like a feast. To *the* feast … to the Wedding Supper of the Lamb.

CHAPTER 6

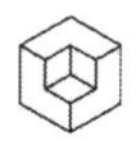

A SPIRIT-FILLED PEOPLE

When they were together for the last time they asked, "Master, are you going to restore the kingdom to Israel now? Is this the time?

He told them, "You don't get to know the time. Timing is the Father's business. What you'll get is the Holy Spirit. And when the Holy Spirit comes on you, you will be able to be my witnesses in Jerusalem, all over Judea and Samaria, even to the ends of the world.

—ACTS 1.6-8

ROUNDING OUT OUR list of five elements we at New Life believe are essential to the concept of "church" is this one: the desire for *all* of the Holy Spirit. To recap where we've been so far, you'll recall that we explored the following four aspects of church:

1. *Jesus is the Center.* Jesus is the "Word" of God—that which God has always and will always be declaring over humanity. Everything we do as a community is aimed at exalting Jesus—the Lord, the Center—knowing that when we do, the world is drawn to his beauty and goodness.
2. *The gospel is for everyone.* Jesus didn't come to save a select few. His life and words and ministry launched a movement that was and is intended for everyone—regardless of their circumstances or station in life. We want our ministry at New Life to speak to everyone—saints, cynics, and prodigals alike.
3. *True discipleship touches the whole life.* Following Jesus makes us part of a *family*, giving us new identity, meaning, and purpose. It gives us a new mission in life and new tasks to accomplish. We become sharers in Jesus' ongoing ministry—both to one another and to the world at large. "*Worship. Connect. Serve.*" This is how we talk about this "whole-life discipleship" at New Life.

4. *We are grounded in a bigger story.* We're not the first people to follow Jesus, and we certainly won't be the last. We've been entrusted with something indescribably precious, which we are called to faithfully hand on to others. We are a people grounded in God's story, in the past, present, and future of what God is doing in the world. The Creed and the Table are the practices that help us honor that grounding.

And then our fifth and final aspect: *We long for the full indwelling of the Holy Spirit.*

. . .

A core conviction of ours at New Life is that it is impossible to follow Jesus apart from the empowerment of his Spirit. No one can hear his voice, respond to his call, or join him in his mission without the enlivening and indwelling presence of the Holy Spirit. Jesus was emphatic about this. The book of Luke records that between his resurrection and his ascension, Jesus gathered a group of disciples around him and said:

> *You can see now how it is written that the Messiah suffers, rises from the dead on the third day, and then a total life-change through the forgiveness of sins is proclaimed in his name to all nations—starting from here, from Jerusalem! You're the first to hear and see it. You're the witnesses. What comes next is very important: I am sending what my Father promised to you, so stay here in the city until he arrives, until you're equipped with power from on high*
> *(Luke 24:46b-49).*

Jesus' words about the "promise" of the Father and "power from on high" are, in fact, one and the same thing; or rather, the same *person*: God the Holy Spirit. In the book of Acts, we read of this Spirit: "When the Holy Spirit comes on you, you will be able to be my witnesses in Jerusalem, all over Judea and Samaria, even to the ends of the world (Acts 1:8).

There's that idea of *empowerment* again, of being "able to" in Christ. Jesus knew that the only hope his disciples had of carrying the resurrection story, the kingdom message, to the ends of the earth; the only hope they had of rising in the midst of history as a "good news" people; the only hope they had of bearing witness in word and deed to God's salvation in a way that drew outsiders to his cause was receiving the empowering presence of God the Holy Spirit.

The Holy Spirit, according to the Scriptures, is the breath of God that *animates* the church; the Holy Spirit makes the church *come alive* as the body of Christ. The Spirit is the wind that blows through the church, sweeping her up into God's kingdom purposes, carrying her into the future that God has for her.

Not surprisingly, in both the Hebrew (the language of the Old Testament) and the Greek (the language of the New Testament), the words that we translate as *Spirit* both mean "wind" or "breath." The Spirit—the *ruach* (Hebrew), the *pneuma* (Greek)—is the "wind" in the sails of the church and the "breath" in the lungs of the church. Without the Spirit we cannot sail. We're as useful as a boat stuck in a harbor. Without the Spirit we cannot *live*. We're as lively as flesh and bone devoid of lungs.

. . .

There's a marvelous scene recorded in the book of Genesis in which God forms Adam, the first human, from the dust of the ground. Once formed, the Scripture says that God *breathed into his nostrils the breath of life* (Genesis 2:7). Without the breath of God, Adam was just a pile of dirt. Beloved of the Lord? Yes. Crafted by the Creator God's own hand? Of course. But did that pile of dirt have any life to speak of? *Not without the breath*.

As it was with Adam, so it is with us. The early believers understood this. And so, following Jesus' ascension, they did what he told them to do: They went back into the city, they gathered regularly for prayer, and then they waited … and waited … and waited …

They waited until the day dawned when the very thing that Jesus said would happen, happened:

> *When the Feast of Pentecost came, they [the church] were all together in one place. Without warning there was a sound like a strong wind, gale force—no one could tell where it came from. It filled the whole building. Then, like a wildfire, the Holy Spirit spread through their ranks, and they started speaking in a number of different languages as the Spirit prompted them (Acts 2:2-4).*

The breath came to those believers' bones. And from that moment on, a movement was launched that would change the world.

Scholars of the early church note that from that group of just one hundred twenty people gathered in the upper room, the church grew rapidly. Several years later, by A.D. 40, there were likely a thousand or so believers; by A.D. 100, seven to ten thousand; by A.D. 200, somewhere north of two *hundred* thousand; and by

A.D. 300, scholars estimate that there were five to six *million* believers spread throughout the Roman Empire![8]

The numbers are staggering when you think about them. It would be fair to call the growth of the early church "rapid" or even "explosive." But maybe the best descriptor of all is "supernatural." The Breath of God poured into the lungs of the first Jesus-followers, filling them up and inspiring their life and witness until the Roman Empire was engulfed in the flame of God's Holy Spirit. Which is exactly what happens when the Spirit of God shows up.

For this reason, many scholars suggest that the book of Acts shouldn't really be thought of primarily as the "acts" of the early church or the apostles, but the "acts" of the Holy Spirit carried out in and through the early church and its apostles. The book of Acts is a powerful testimony to the dynamic working of God the Holy Spirit *through* the church. Healings and other miracles; prophetic preaching followed by mass conversions; male and female, slave and free, young and old, Jew and Gentile coming together to form a new community … all of it is the work of the God the Holy Spirit.

. . .

It should come as no surprise that whenever we read through the letters of the New Testament (all of which were written by apostles to churches that sprung to life during the time period described in the book of Acts), everything seems very "Spirit-saturated." Consider just a few examples:

---

[8] Noted by Larry Hurtado in *Destroyer of the Gods* (Waco: Baylor University Press, 2016), 3.

- The Holy Spirit touches our spirits and confirms who we are as children of the Father (see Romans 8:15).
- The Holy Spirit compels us to abandon individualistic living in favor of becoming part of the body of Christ (see 1 Corinthians 12:13).
- The Holy Spirit equips us with spiritual gifts to serve one another in love (see the entirety of 1 Corinthians 12).
- The Holy Spirit causes us to grow in kingdom virtues (see Galatians 5:22-23).
- The Holy Spirit pours the love of God into our hearts, filling us with hope (see Romans 5:5).
- The Holy Spirit helps us pray when we don't know what or how to pray (see Romans 8:26).
- The Holy Spirit serves as the "pledge" of the good future that God promises to us (see Ephesians 1:13-14).

The point is this: There is no good thing that God wants to do for us or give to us, nothing that he desires for us to be or to accomplish, nothing that he's called us to or purposed us for that does not come to us by way of the person of the Holy Spirit. And so we set our desire on the Holy Spirit. We want all that he is and all that God the Father desires to give us through him. Paul said to the believers gathered at Ephesus, "Drink the Spirit of God" (Ephesians 5:18). Given that he was writing this to a group of believers, it's fair to assume that Paul's audience had *already* tasted and been filled with the Spirit of God. The implication, then, is that believers are to drink … and drink … and keep on drinking the Spirit—again and again and again.

We should *never* stop opening our lives to the Holy Spirit of God. Which is why at New Life we welcome his powerful presence. God longs to inundate both our church corporately and our lives individually *fully and continually* with his Holy Spirit. From there his intention is to inundate our city, our state, and our world with his presence. He is building a home, remember, whose roof will cover the whole world—the heavens and the earth. He's building a center of worship that is on fire with the flame of God's love.

And so we plead with God the Holy Spirit to give us grace and to show us Jesus afresh, and to teach us anew what it means to love him and those around us with our whole hearts. We ask that through our worship in song and the teaching of the Word and our coming to the Table, the Holy Spirit would show us the beauty and holiness and glory of God in ways that we've never seen before, drawing us into the mystery of how God is with us for our good, forever, in Christ the Lord. We pray that there is not one second of any meeting we lead, any event we organize, or any worship service we host where the Holy Spirit is not joyfully welcomed, where our hearts are not standing on the edge, waiting for him to come.

. . .

One of the oldest prayers of the church is also perhaps the simplest. It goes like this: "*Come, Holy Spirit ...*"

Isn't that wonderful? The earliest followers of Jesus prayed this prayer with regularity and in so doing extended an invitation for the Holy Spirit to make himself known. As the Creed says, he is "The Lord, the Giver of Life." When we pray that prayer, we're saying, *"Arise among us, Lord and Life-Giver. We need you. We're dry bones without you. We're desperate for your presence, for your power, for you."*

English sea captain Sir Francis Drake, who lived in the 16th century, was the second person to circumnavigate the globe. He wrote a prayer that captured his desire to live adventurously before the Lord, and his words serve as a brilliant statement of how we at New Life Church desire to live as a community. It reads:

Disturb us, Lord, when
We are too pleased with ourselves,
When our dreams have come true
Because we dreamed too little,
When we arrived safely
Because we sailed too close to the shore.

Disturb us, Lord, when
With the abundance of things we possess
We have lost our thirst
For the waters of life;
Having fallen in love with life,
We have ceased to dream of eternity
And in our efforts to build a new earth,
We have allowed our vision
Of the new Heaven to dim.

Disturb us, Lord, to dare more boldly,
To venture on wilder seas
Where storms will show Your mastery;
Where losing sight of land,
We shall find the stars.

We ask you to push back
The horizons of our hopes;

And to push back the future
In strength, courage, hope, and love.

This we ask in the name of our Captain,
Who is Jesus Christ.

"Disturb us"—what a bold prayer to pray. Indeed, there is a sense in which the Holy Spirit is the great *Disturber,* the great *Agitator* of our lives. Nestled safely in the harbor, moored to the dock, it's easy to feel like we've got it made. And then we notice that the winds begin to pick up, that the water becomes choppy, and we turn our heads just in time to see Jesus, our Captain, loosening the ropes of our boat from the dock.

"What are you doing?!" we cry, as he silently looks skyward to welcome the Wind of his Father. That Wind blows us out beyond our self-made safety and into the great, wild adventure of the kingdom. We know not where we are going, but we trust the Spirit who blows in our sails, the Son who captains the vessel, and the Father who has beckoned us into the journey to begin with.

This is who we long to be as a community, as a church. We want to live adventurously with the Spirit. We want to give in a way that stretches our faith, and serve in a way that expands our love, and pray in a way that causes our hearts to buckle with ache for our city. And so we beg God

for vision that requires faith we don't yet have,
for dreams that take us way beyond our comfort,
and for fresh, kingdom-shaped desires that make blood race through our veins.

"Come, Holy Spirit! Disturb us. We're waiting here, for you."

. . .

What does this look like, specifically? Well, perhaps you'll notice it in the way that people *pray* around here. From small group leaders to section leaders to pastors (whether in one-on-one visits or from the platform), prayer is not a chore. It's not a box to check out of religious obligation so that God will give us gold stars. No, for us it's a real interaction with the living God in which we invite him to disturb our lives.

You'll notice it in the way that we *worship.* Whether that worship takes place in living rooms, in kids' classrooms, in our Sunday gatherings, or in special services that we host, you'll notice that our worship is full of life and passion. Do you know why? Because we believe that God the Spirit stands on the edge of readiness, eager to flood us with life, aching to challenge us in fresh ways. So, we worship in the same way that we pray: *to lean into the presence of the Spirit all the more.*

You'll notice it in our *preaching and teaching.* Once again, at every level of our community's life you will see that this is so. From small groups to Sunday morning classes, from our elementary school classrooms to our student ministries, from our Spanish-speaking congregation to Sundays at our North campus, you'll feel it—our preachers and teachers are "contending for the Spirit," asking the Spirit to *come.*

Preaching and teaching, for us, is not about *merely* transmitting biblical knowledge—it is about the prophetic message of Jesus Christ racing out from the mouth of the preacher, shattering every resistance, bringing the kingdom. Our preachers and teachers believe in their bones: *We can't do this without the Holy*

Spirit. We know that if he doesn't show up, nothing of substance will happen.

So, again: We welcome him. We make room for the Great Disturber.

But do you know where you'll notice it most if you have eyes to see? In Galatians 5:22-23, the apostle Paul listed the "fruits," or evidences, of the Spirit's work. They are:

love
joy
peace
forbearance
kindness
goodness
faithfulness
gentleness
self-control

It is possible to miss the genuinely *supernatural* because we were fixated on the *spectacular*. Hang around New Life long enough and you'll see plenty of "spectacular." But more often and more consistent and really, no less spectacular when you think about it), is the *supernatural* work of God the Holy Spirit: Present in the deep, affectionate, sacrificial love that people who were once strangers now miraculously share with one another …

Present in the joyful clamor in our hallways and living rooms, in the hooting and hollering of our children before and after services, in the smiles written on the faces of our worshipers …

Present in the peace-filled relationships Christ Jesus is forging among us, in the bonds of love that are healing our lives and making us whole …

God the Holy Spirit is *everywhere* among us, filling us with life, making the riches of the triune God available to us, here and now, in space and time. Which is why the Creed says that the Holy Spirit is the Lord, the Giver of Life who proceeds from the Father [and the Son], who with the Father and the Son is worshiped and glorified … He has spoken through the Prophets.

God the Holy Spirit—blessed be he.

. . .

At the outset of this book, we looked at a passage from Matthew 16 regarding Jesus' commitment to building his church, a church so strong and resilient that even the gates of hell would not prevail against it. And we have outlined what we at New Life believe is required to further that vision of Christ's—what is *essential* to our being a people who faithfully bear his name and embody his character. Our hope is that you will find this vision so compelling that you would come link arms with us, joining your efforts with those of countless others who have similarly been gripped by the goodness and beauty of Jesus' love.

The reward for us is detailed in the passage from Matthew 16. "You will have complete and free access to God's kingdom," Jesus declared to his disciples, and also to us, "keys to open any and every door" (v. 19).

Jesus' invitation to "follow me" opens the world to us. It introduces us to God's transforming grace, incorporates us into a life-giving family, and gives us a new hope and a better future: the present and coming kingdom of God.

Made in the USA
Middletown, DE
18 September 2018